LIGHTNING

LIGHTNING

PETER MURRAY

THE CHILD'S WORLD®, INC.

Photo Credits

Weatherstock/Warren Faidley: cover, 2, 6, 10, 13, 15, 16, 19, 20, 23, 24, 26, 29, 30
Weatherstock/Lawrence M. Sawyer: 9

Printed in the United States of America.

Library of Congress Cataloging-in-Publication Data
Murray, Peter, 1952 Sept. 29-
Lightning/Peter Murray.
p.   cm.
Includes index.
Summary: Explains how lightning forms and the impact it can have.
ISBN 1-56766-215-3 (hard cover : Library binding)
1. Lightning--Juvenile literature.   [1. Lightning.]
I. Title.
QC966.5.M87   1996
551.5'632--dc20   95-45342
                          CIP
                          AC

TABLE OF CONTENTS

It is a hot summer day. The sky is mostly blue, but you see some clouds above the western horizon. The tops of the clouds are huge puffs of white reaching high into the sky. The bottom layer is dark gray, almost black. In a few minutes, the dark clouds block the sun. Wind whips through the trees, tearing off leaves.

The clouds are lit by flashes of lightning. A few seconds later comes the crash of thunder. As the storm approaches, the lightning and thunder come closer together. Suddenly, a huge, incredibly bright lightning bolt hits a tree. You hear a tremendous crackle and a boom so loud the windows rattle.

Storm clouds appear in the sky.

The flash was so bright that when you close your eyes, you can still see it. You look out the window again. Something doesn't look right. The tree is split in half, and it is smoking.

Lightning is one of nature's most powerful forces. It can destroy buildings and trees. It can kill people and animals. It can start fires. A single bolt is hotter than the surface of the sun. When lightning strikes, nothing is safe!

Lightning splits a tree.

Lightning is a sudden, violent movement of electrons. **Electrons** are very tiny, negatively charged particles. They are even smaller than atoms. Electricity is the study of how electrons move. When electrons move through a metal wire, they are invisible. But when they jump through the air, we see a spark. The electrons heat the air and make it glow.

Lightning is a giant electric spark.

Lightning is caused by a violent movement of electrons

WHAT CAUSES LIGHTNING?

To make an electric spark, you need electricity. But how does electricity get into the clouds? Thunderclouds are made of ice crystals and water droplets, all swirling around each other. Water droplets are blown up to the top of the cloud, where it is very cold. They freeze into hailstones. The hailstones fall and crash into each other. This movement gives the hail a negative electrical charge. At the top of the cloud, the smaller ice crystals are left with a positive electrical charge.

When the natural electricity in the cloud is out of balance, something has to happen.

Lightning occurs when the electricity in a cloud is out of balance.

The negatively charged electrons in the bottom of the cloud are pulled toward the positively charged particles in the top of the cloud. In a sudden burst of heat and light, a stream of electrons moves from one part of the cloud to the other. This single lightning bolt might be several miles long and contain 156 quintillion electrons!

Lightning helps restore the natural electrical balance in the clouds.

The positive and negative electrons in a cloud form lightning.

Sometimes a positive electrical charge builds up on the ground. That makes the electrons in the thundercloud discharge into the earth. This type of lightning is the most dangerous. Most of this cloud-to-ground lightning strikes tall objects such as trees and buildings. You should never stand under a tree during a thunderstorm! The best place to be is inside a car or a building.

Some people say that lightning never strikes the same place twice. They are wrong! The Empire State Building in New York City is struck by lightning several times a year.

Lightning hits a tower on top of a mountain.

WHAT DOES LIGHTNING LOOK LIKE?

When we see a bolt of lightning, it looks like a jagged bar of light. It flashes for less than a second, then it is gone. But if we could see the lightning in slow motion, it would look very different.

First, a thin stream of electrons, as big around as a piece of string, shoots down from the clouds. Electrons travel best in moist air, so the stream zig-zags this way and that, following the wettest places in the air. The electron stream branches off, like the limbs of an upside-down tree. This branching electron stream is called a **stepped leader**.

Lightning looks like a jagged bar of light.

As the stepped leader gets closer to the ground, a stream of positively charged particles rises to meet it. This is called an **upward streamer**. When the two streams meet, look out! A lightning channel has formed. It is only an inch across, but billions upon billions of electrons race through it. They heat up the air and everything else in their path.

A lighting channel forms from a storm cloud.

WHAT IS THUNDER?

The sudden heat of the lightning makes the moist air explode outward. This explosion makes the sound we call **thunder**. Every lightning flash makes its own thunder. And every time you hear thunder, it has been caused by lightning.

You can use thunder to tell how far you are from a lightning flash. The light from the flash reaches your eyes in much less than a second. The sound from thunder travels slower. When you see the lightning, count the number of seconds it takes to hear the thunder. Every five seconds counts as one mile.

Every lightning flash makes thunder.

ARE THERE OTHER KINDS OF LIGHTNING?

Not all lightning looks like jagged, forked bolts. If lightning is very far away, it might look as though someone is playing with a giant flashlight above the clouds. The lightning is too far away for us to hear the thunder. Some people call this **heat lightning**, because it is often seen on hot summer nights.

Ribbon lightning sometimes occurs during windy storms. The wind spreads out the lightning channel, making it wider. Ribbon lightning looks like a wide, striped ribbon.

Ribbon lightning appears during violent, windy storms.

The most mysterious lightning of all is **ball lightning**. Ball lightning is very rare. It looks like a glowing ball the size of a melon, floating through the air. You never know what ball lightning will do. It might go up, it might go down, it might roll along the ground, or it might come drifting in through a window. Usually ball lightning quietly fades away after a few seconds. But sometimes it disappears with a loud BANG!

Ball lightning sometimes appears after a lightning strike—but not very often. You never know when ball lightning will occur.

Ball lightning is very rare.

CAN LIGHTNING MAKE GLASS?

When lightning strikes a sandy area, it sometimes leaves behind curious objects called **fulgurites**. The lightning bolt is pulled deep into the sand, and the heat from the bolt melts the sand into glass. Fulgurites show us the shape of the lightning channel as it shoots through the sand. Some fulgurites are more than six feet long!

Fulgurites are formed when lightning hits a sandy area.

Lightning is important to our planet. It keeps the Earth's electrical field in balance. It also helps us in other ways. Every lightning bolt produces ozone gas. The ozone rises into the atmosphere and becomes part of the the Earth's ozone layer. **Ozone** helps protect us from the sun's radiation. Lightning also helps clean our air. Pollution particles become electrically charged and fall to the Earth.

Without lightning, we might not even be here. Scientists believe that the first forms of life on Earth may have been created by lightning strikes.

Fires caused by lightning help keep the planets ecosystem in balance.

GLOSSARY

ball lightning (BALL LITE-ning)
A rare kind of lightning that forms a ball that can roll along the ground or even float in the air.

electrons (ee-LECK-trons)
Very tiny, negatively charged particles.

fulgurites (FULL-gurr-ites)
Long, oddly shaped blobs of glass formed when lightning strikes sand and melts it.

heat lightning (HEET LITE ning)
Lightning that is very far away, so that it just looks like light flashing among the clouds.

ozone (OH-zone)
An invisible gas formed by lighting. It helps to protect the earth from the sun's rays.

ribbon lightning (RIB-un LITE-ning)
A wide bolt of lightning caused when strong wind spreads out the electron stream.

stepped leader (stept LEE-der)
The jagged, branching stream of electrons that shoots down from the clouds.

thunder (THUN-der)
The loud, rumbling noise caused by lighting. The sudden heat produced by a lightning bolt makes the moist air around it explode, causing a loud noise.

upward streamer (UP-wurd STREEM-er)
A stream of positively charged particles that rises from the ground, to meet the stream traveling down from the clouds.

INDEX